ALTERNATOR BOOKS™

UNDERSTANDING AI

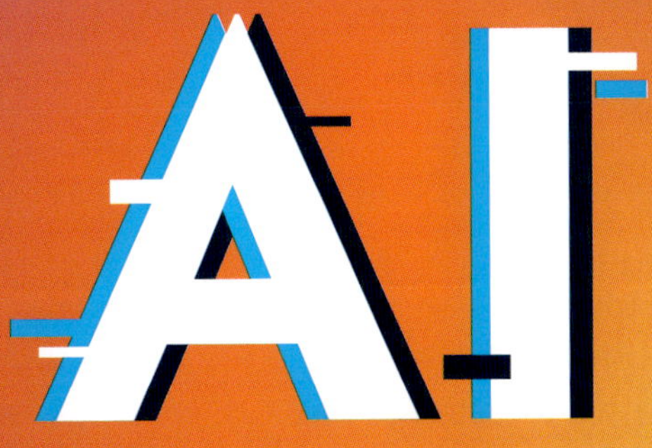

Katie Clark

Lerner Publications ◆ Minneapolis

Dedicated to my loves, always.

Lerner Publications Company
An imprint of Lerner Publishing Group, Inc.
241 First Avenue North
Minneapolis, MN 55401 USA

For reading levels and more information, look up this title at www.lernerbooks.com.

Main body text set in Aptifer Sans LT Pro
Typeface provided by Linotype.

Library of Congress Cataloging-in-Publication Data

Names: Clark, Katie, 1983–author
Title: Understanding AI / Katie Clark.
Description: Minneapolis, MN : Lerner Publications, [2026] | Series: Digital safety smarts (alternator books) | Includes bibliographical references and index. | Audience term: juvenile | Audience: Ages 8–12 Lerner Publications | Audience: Grades 4–6 Lerner Publications | Summary: "The use of artificial intelligence is on the rise and the programs are always evolving. Readers will learn how AI utilizes machine learning, and how to responsibly employ AI tools as a creative jumping-off point"—Provided by publisher.
Identifiers: LCCN 2024047639 (print) | LCCN 2024047640 (ebook) | ISBN 9798765668283 library binding | ISBN 9798765683866 paperback | ISBN 9798765676530 epub
Subjects: LCSH: Artificial intelligence—Juvenile literature
Classification: LCC Q335.4 .C53 2026 (print) | LCC Q335.4 (ebook) | DDC 006.3—dc23/eng/20250131

LC record available at https://lccn.loc.gov/2024047639
LC ebook record available at https://lccn.loc.gov/2024047640

Manufactured in the United States of America
1-CG- 7/15/25

TABLE OF CONTENTS

A BAD IDEA

Sadie plopped into her seat on the bus. Her friend Kate was already there. "What are you doing tonight?" Kate asked.

"Tomorrow's Wednesday. I have to write a report for Miss Baker's class that I haven't started," Sadie said. "Should I write about the Constitution or the Declaration of Independence?"

Kate scrunched up her nose. "Boring. You should come to the roller-skating rink with me instead."

Sadie bit her lip. She had been looking at an AI writing tool online that she wanted to try. Maybe she could use it to write her report, but using AI to do assignments was against school policy. Would Miss Baker notice?

"Okay, I'll ask my mom," she said.

The next day, Sadie laid the report on Miss Baker's desk and hurried to her seat. She fidgeted as she found it hard to sit still.

Using AI can seem quick and easy, but it should never be used to complete homework or projects for you.

Why am I so nervous, anyway? she wondered. *Teachers probably can't even tell if their students used AI.*

On Friday, as she took her seat in history class, she noticed Miss Baker looking at her.

Her hands shook slightly as Miss Baker approached a few minutes later.

"Can I talk to you at my desk?" Miss Baker asked quietly.

Uh-oh.

Sadie followed her teacher to the front of the class while everyone else did a worksheet. Miss Baker showed her the report, and she said she could tell Sadie had not written it herself.

With flaming hot cheeks, Sadie admitted she had used an AI tool. She also promised never to do it again. As she returned to her seat, she couldn't help thinking what a bad idea it had been.

WHAT IS AI?

Have you ever heard of something called artificial intelligence, or AI? Have you heard of people using AI to write reports, articles, or books? Or maybe you've seen an image online that looks too perfect or too bizarre to be real. These experiences can leave a person wondering how it was created. What is AI, anyway?

How Does It Work?

Artificial intelligence is a type of technology that teaches computers and machines how to act like humans. AI allows them to learn, solve problems, make decisions, and even be creative on their own.

How does it work? How can a non-human program understand a human's questions or commands? How can it create detailed art or write a book report about American history?

People create AI programs. The AI programs learn from data. This data doesn't come out of thin air! The developers

AI requires large amounts of technology stored in places called data centers. These centers use a lot of energy and resources to keep AI working correctly.

collect an incredible amount of information from human research, experiences, and observations. Then they code the programs in a way that lets the AI understand the data and give a response.

AI programs are able to use data and algorithms to learn like a human, and this helps them learn to give more right answers over time. This is called machine learning. The programs take the information that is available to them and generate responses that the algorithms determine will be correct. This lets them do things like write a report about animals.

Humans shape the way that AI programs use data and information.

The Many Uses of AI

Why do people create these programs in the first place? AI can be used in a lot of helpful ways. Artists and writers can use AI to inspire them. Scientists, healthcare workers, and government offices often use AI too. They can use it to make predictions relating to safety, health, or nature. The programs make predictions based on past human studies and experiences they've learned about.

When used correctly, AI can be a great tool! It can cut down on the time needed to perform many tasks, and it can often see patterns that humans might miss.

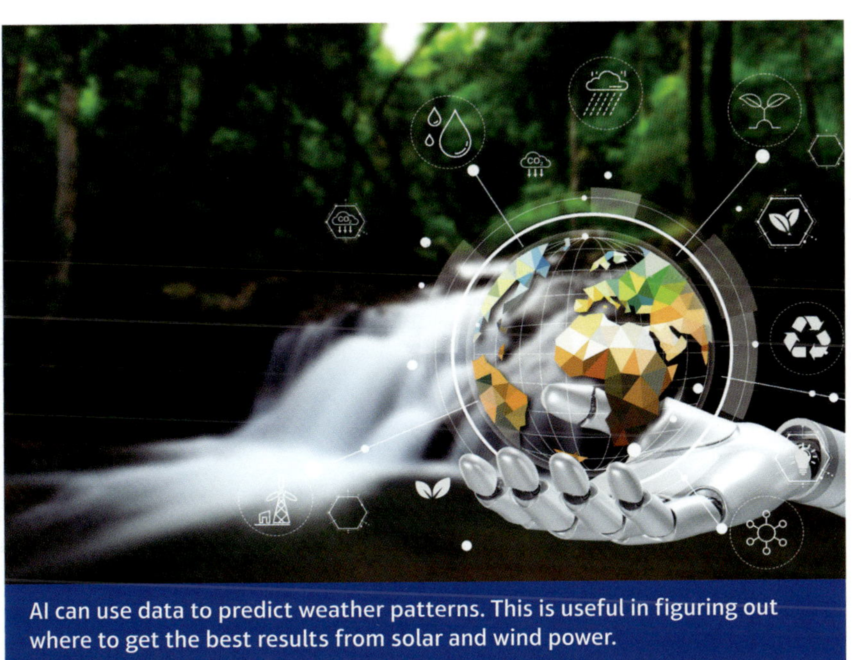

AI can use data to predict weather patterns. This is useful in figuring out where to get the best results from solar and wind power.

FUN AI FACTS

☞ Device assistants like Siri and Alexa use AI to figure out what we want when we give them a command.

☞ Online shops use AI to guess what consumers want to buy based on their previous purchases.

☞ AI generators can be used to create artwork, music, books, and movies.

☞ Climate and wildlife scientists use AI to make predictions about our planet and how to keep it healthy.

☞ Teachers can use AI to help students learn languages, master technology, and more!

AI All Around Us

Believe it or not, most of us use some form of AI every single day. Wondering if you've ever used it? If you have ever typed something into an internet search engine, such as Google, the answer is yes!

The same goes for using word prediction in text messages or asking an app for directions. AI is also used in programs like video streaming services or even in weather prediction.

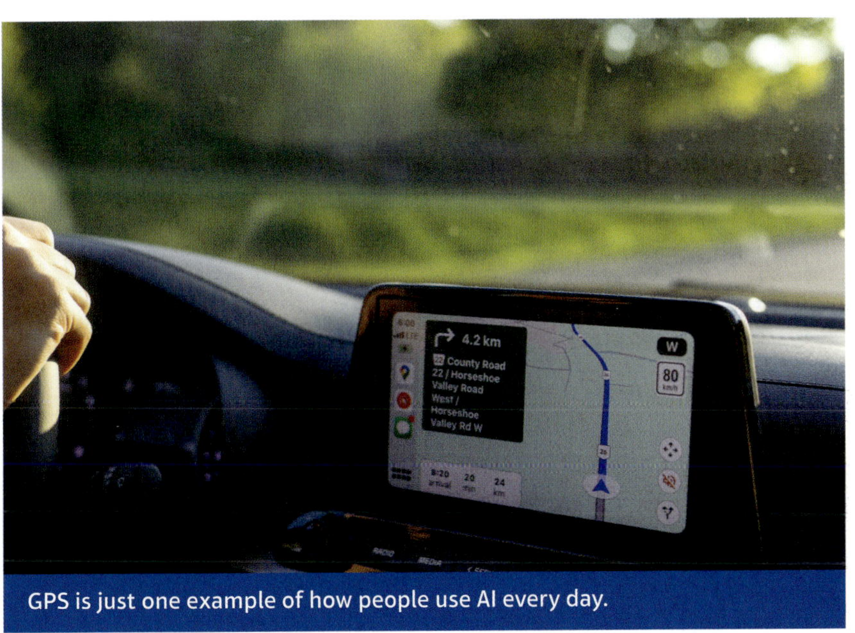

GPS is just one example of how people use AI every day.

CHAPTER TWO

AI ETHICS AND BIAS

It's important to use AI ethically. This means to use it fairly and to accepted standards. It's also important to avoid bias and using AI results that are not accurate. You might be wondering how. Let's find out!

Ethical AI Use

Using artificial intelligence can be great, but as Sadie learned earlier, it can also be unethical when used the wrong way. Here are a few examples of improper, or unethical, AI use.

- taking credit for something you didn't create
- stealing a creator's content and selling it as your own
- using AI to edit images to spread lies or rumors

On the other hand, there are a lot of great ways AI can help, encourage, and benefit others.

- predicting the best outcome for medicine or healthcare procedures

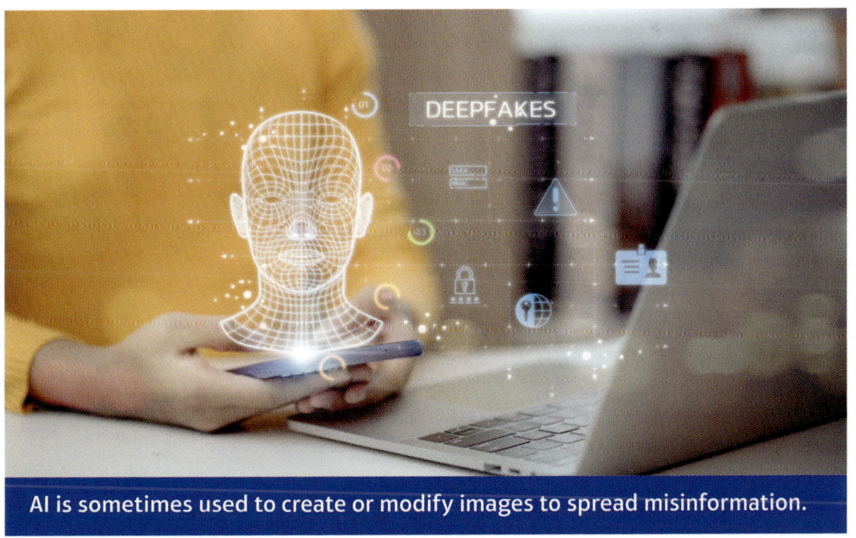

AI is sometimes used to create or modify images to spread misinformation.

- giving writing prompts to get started on school projects
- predicting best practices and routes for safety patrols

What Is Bias?

Artificial intelligence uses information it gets from humans. Since humans make mistakes, that means AI can too.

AI MILESTONES

AI has come a long way! From the first neural network in 1957, to a chess-playing supercomputer in 1996, to generative AIs such as Google's Gemini in 2023 and Apple Intelligence in 2024, plus many more.

The machine learning process needs complete information to help avoid bias.

This happens when programmers do not have complete information. Bias is an error that occurs due to wrong assumptions in the machine learning process. For example, if a researcher is trying to decide whether the majority of people like blue or red better, they might do a survey. They might ask one hundred people if they like red or blue better.

If every person says red, the researcher might determine that everyone on the planet likes the color red better than the color blue. The researcher would then program the AI to say that everyone likes red better than blue.

Does this mean it is true? Not really. This is a wrong assumption. Maybe the researcher didn't find anyone who liked blue best because they didn't ask enough people, or because they only asked people with red shirts.

There are a number of ways that bias can affect peoples' lives if it is allowed to creep into AI programming.

This is an example of incomplete information which leads to bias.

Bias can lead to information that expresses a certain point of view. You might be wondering why it matters. Imagine if an AI that was trained with biased information was asked to write a law or a contract. This could lead to someone being hurt or discriminated against due to incomplete information.

Being ethical means using AI in a way that is right and fair.

CRITICAL THINKING

Since we can't always know if what AI predicts is correct, how can a person tell what's true or false? The answer to this is by using critical thinking skills. These skills can help us use common sense when something seems a bit fishy.

What Is Critical Thinking?

Critical thinking is a way of thinking that lets you question and evaluate what you are being told. Developing this skill can really come in handy! It will help you discern between fake news and real information. It can help you tell the difference between real images and images that have been edited or changed to bully or trick someone.

Uncovering AI Writing

The best way to use critical thinking is to ask questions. If, for example, the grammar seems strange and you suspect

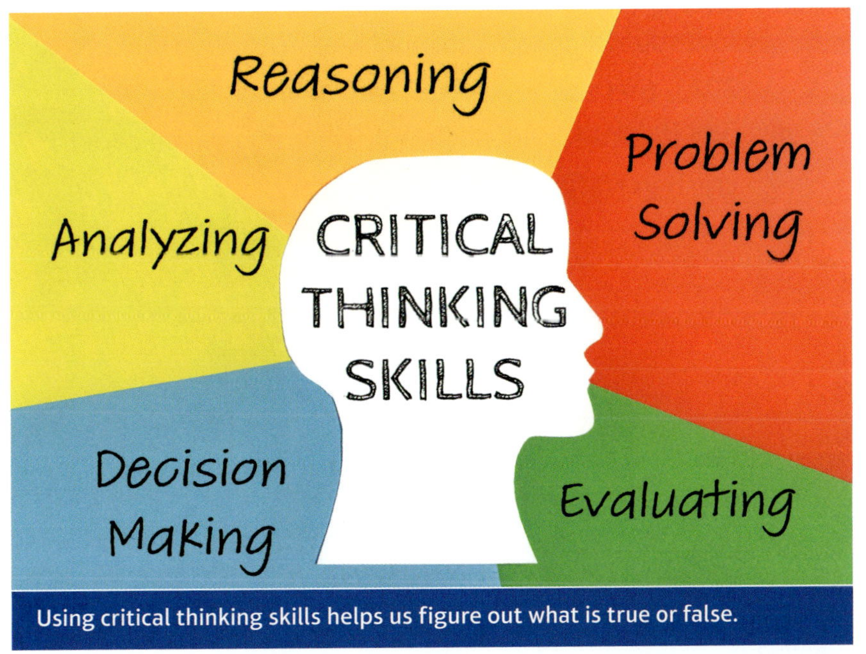

Using critical thinking skills helps us figure out what is true or false.

Dangers of AI

AI is not foolproof. One big AI failure involved Tesla, a brand that makes electric cars. Tesla's Autopilot feature uses multiple cameras and sensors to see the car's surroundings so AI can drive the car. An investigation into Autopilot found that from 2021 to 2023, there were at least thirteen cases where the vehicle's Autopilot AI failed. This caused the cars to crash in traffic, killing the drivers.

AI is to blame, dig further with specific questions. Did this information come from a reliable source? Do other websites agree with this information?

Spotting AI Images

When someone shows you an image, can you tell if it was made by AI? Here are a few tips to help spot the difference!

Look for things that don't belong, like a finger in the wrong place or a strange bend of the light. You can also

AI is often not great at making hands and fingers, so that is a good place to start when trying to determine if an image is created by AI.

IMPORTANT QUESTIONS TO ASK ABOUT CONTENT MADE BY AI:

 When was this content created? Is it recent or is the information outdated?

 Does the information or image match what you would expect to find?

 Where does the information come from? Is it a reliable and accurate source?

 Is it biased by someone trying to sell or convince you of something with the information?

look at the edges of the objects in the photo. Are they oddly smooth or sharp? Any of these clues can help you determine if a picture was created by an AI program.

When it comes to using information from an AI source, ask as many questions as you can think of to verify it.

USING AI
RESPONSIBLY

From the invention of AI in the 1950s to the many amazing artificial intelligence programs of today, we are lucky to have this tool at our fingertips. As with all technology, we must use it responsibly. But what does this mean?

Don't Use AI for Bad

Using AI responsibly can mean lots of different things. It is important to remember to never use AI to bully anyone. Don't ever take a picture of someone and edit it to make it embarrassing. Likewise, never create a fake image of someone doing something that could get them in trouble.

AI technology makes it possible to replace the face of a person in an image to make it look like someone else was doing what is shown in the image.

It is also a good idea to take a cue from Sadie's story at the beginning of this book. Don't use AI to cheat on your homework and claim you created the AI's content, or to plagiarize someone else's work.

AI programs can sometimes plagiarize writing or art, so it's important to double check anything it generates.

Use AI for Good!

Do you want to use AI the right way? Try using it as a starting point for some great ideas. Ask it to give you writing prompts to get inspired when working on reports, music, or art.

Be sure to edit AI content and add your own personal touches. Sprinkle in your own voice and experiences. If you're creating AI art, add different colors, graphics, and illustrations that are all your own.

CREATIVE AI TOOLS

AI tools aren't one-size-fits-all! They can do many things, such as video editing, writing, creating art, coding, audio editing, and more. AI capabilities and its range of uses continue to expand quickly every year.

Looking to the Future

Artificial intelligence is constantly evolving. It is being used in art, education, healthcare, government, business, and more. Learning about it today can help you be one step ahead tomorrow. It may seem scary at times, but if we use it responsibly, it can help us make the world a better place.

What sorts of new uses could you think of for AI?

AI can be used on most devices, from smartphones to laptops and more.

As the use of AI continues to grow, care must be taken to use it responsibly.

GLOSSARY

algorithm: a step-by-step way to solve a problem or come to a decision

assumption: a fact or statement taken for granted

bias: errors in a computer program that lead to unfair or wrong outcomes

code: to put in or into form or symbols

critical thinking: a way of thinking that lets you question and evaluate information

data: the collection of information for statistics, values, and facts

developer: someone who creates or produces software

discriminate: to treat some people better than others without any fair or proper reason

ethical: acting in a way that is fair and right

generative AI: a type of technology that can produce content such as writing and art

neural network: a computer architecture in which processors are interconnected in a way that looks like the connections between neurons in a human brain, and which is able to learn by a process of trial and error

plagiarize: to copy from someone else and call it one's own

LEARN MORE

Britannica Kids: Artificial Intelligence
https://kids.britannica.com/kids/article/artificial-intelligence
/390648

Hutchinson, Sam. *Artificial Intelligence Activity Book: Activities about Computers, AI, and Machine Learning.* New York: Racehorse, 2024.

Inspirit Scholars: AI For Kids
https://www.inspiritscholars.com/blog/what-is-ai-for-kids/

Kiddie: Artificial Intelligence Facts for Kids
https://kids.kiddle.co/Artificial_intelligence

Newland, Sonya. *Brainy Computers.* London, England: Wayland, 2021.

Oxlade, Chris. *Computer Science for Curious Kids: An Illustrated Introduction to Software Programming, Artificial Intelligence, Cyber Security, and More!* London, England: Arcturus, 2023.

Pitara: What is Artificial Intelligence?
https://www.pitara.com/science-for-kids/5ws-and-h/what-is
-artificial-intelligence/

Verr, Paul. *The Brainiac's Book of Robots and AI.* London, England: Thames & Hudson, 2023.

INDEX

PHOTO ACKNOWLEDGMENTS

Image credits: Dean Drobot/Shutterstock, p. 5; Make more Aerials/Shutterstock, p. 7; Owlie Productions/Shutterstock, p. 8; tonton/Shutterstock, p. 9; Yana Vasylyshena/Shutterstock, p. 11; CL STOCK/Shutterstock, p. 13; Shutterstock AI Generator, p. 14; Wright Studio/Shutterstock, p. 15; Summit Art Creations/Shutterstock, p. 16; travellight/Shutterstock, p.17; Andrii Sumandaq/Shutterstock, p. 19; Shutterstock AI, p. 21; Oko Laa/Shutterstock, p. 23; Monkey MDV Edwards/Shutterstock, p. 25; Jakkrit Orrasri/Shutterstock, p. 26; GamePixel/Shutterstock, p. 27; BearFotos/Shutterstock, p. 28; PeopleImages.com - Yuri A/Shutterstock, p. 29; Just dance/Shutterstock, p. 31. Cover image: AU USAnakul/Shutterstock.